ARTISTIC CHILDREN BREATHE DIFFERENTLY

ARTISTIC CHILDREN BREATHE DIFFERENTLY

A Chapbook

Eve Wood

Hollyridge Press
Venice, California

© 2005 Eve Wood

All rights reserved under International and Pan-American Copyright Conventions. Published in the United States by Hollyridge Press.

Hollyridge Press
P.O. Box 2872
Venice, California 90294
www.hollyridgepress.com

Cover and Book Design by Rio Smyth
Author Photo by Brian Deutsch
Manufactured in the United States of America by Lightning Source

ISBN-13: 978-0-9752573-4-0
ISBN-10: 0-9752573-4-X

Grateful acknowledgment is made to the editors of the following publications where these poems first appeared:

The Greensboro Review: "I would like to marry you, but I won't"
Nightsun: "Whiteness"
Witness: "Queen Anne Cherries"
Karamu: "Lesson Plan For A New Day"
The Florida Review: "About The River"

Contents

So Many Questions, So Close To Home	3
The Recklessness of Water	4
Nothing	5
Responsibility	6
Equinox of The Flamethrower	7
Early This Morning	8
Lesson Plan For A New Day	9
Epilepsy Late In Life	11
Blood In The Chocolate, Chocolate In The Blood	12
Translation	13
Whiteness	14
About The River	15
Woman With Bread Crumbs	17
And The Paper, And The Pen	19
Inscriptions In A Dark Room	20
Mistakes	21
My Father's Pen	22
Artistic Children Breathe Differently	23
Against Parenting	24
I Would Like To Marry You, But I Won't	25
Queen Anne Cherries	27
Pots	28
Apples In My Heart	29
Wonderful	30
Only The Ruptured Eye Sees What Must Be Done	31
Just Maybe	32
The Need For Everything	34
Chopping Walnuts	35
Words Before Leaving	36
The True Meaning Of *Yes*	37

Artistic Children Breathe Differently

SO MANY QUESTIONS, SO CLOSE TO HOME

Yes, said the river. The river said *yes*.
I only know this because I was standing
by the river without my shoes,
and the water slipped, thin and tight.
The *yes*, when it came, was cold,
but still a *yes* is better than *maybe*.
I walked back toward the field,
believing the river's *yes* belonged to everything,
and everything would love me.
But a *yes* is just a *no*, sanctified.
The stones would not break their permanent *no*,
like an echo in winter.
I thought if I placed them on my tongue
they might soften,
but no.
The reeds in the wind, a *maybe*, then a *yes*, then a *no*,
then a *maybe*, then a *yes*, then a *yes*,
then *no*.
Could be, said the oak, though you'll never know for sure,
and the birch tree only wanted to be touched
by a wide, kind hand.
The wind said everything all at once,
and I was too sad to ask again.
Yes, said the river, when I came back,
and the river asked why I came back,
and I did not say *yes* right away,
but then I said it.
Yes. I did.

THE RECKLESSNESS OF WATER

Not the water but the shore
where stunned into anxious movement
at the sight of his body moon drenched naked
as though an orchestra sat playing on the surface of the lake
I would not let myself go
Not the shore but the precipice
where I staggered for reasons
unknown to me
Not the precipice but the distance
between his hands as he reached for my body
Not the distance but the trees
their stirrings their watchfulness
over our bodies
Not the trees but the embankment
where pieces of grass collected between his fingers
and mud like a salve on his chest and thighs
Not the embankment but the moon behind his head
as he leaned in to kiss my open mouth
Not the moon but the indentation in his chin
as though God shot an arrow that would not go through
Not the indentation but the face itself
the solidity the belief in nothing and everything at once
Not the face itself but the eyes behind the face
coming to terms with all they see and how they see it
Yes the eyes behind the face
the storm that welled up in them
the recklessness of water spilling over me

NOTHING

I don't believe in the swan dead on the highway,
Its neck, a slender loop
Where the edge of the water rises
To land.
She is there,
Her body diminished, blunt and sad.
On the way to the library, a wren on its side,
And the place in the sky from which the bird fell
Offers nothing.

Somewhere a person sits having a birthday,
And five pigeons dead in the length of a city block,
And the glasses raised, not with admiration
But mistrust
For nothing can be fully taken in.

Time passes, a slow flood.
Hawks are not shot from the sky,
But commit themselves to falling,
And the clouds no longer take stock of the gull.

The surface of a lake shivers with the cry of something
Large and hopeful, a bear maybe,
Or the loon, come back for luck.

Nothing ever goes away.
The small, reedy finch waivers,
But the branch doesn't break.
Nothing obvious happens,
But by morning she is gone.

RESPONSIBILITY

The bright wreath of existence shines open,
And each hour ticks its pact
Until one day the bargaining stops.
Lying, words become part
Of the ear that hears them.
Thoughts masticate the air
Turning in on themselves in warm circles,
The knowledge that all I betray
Comes back,
And isn't responsibility a quickening toward death,
A commitment forged in silence,
Veiled and rapturous?
A bell rings inside the most difficult moments,
To clarify the mystery of what was once left behind.
I move like a gray blade set to motion.
I fix and release to fix hard again.
Doesn't it mean everything to finally learn
What it takes to let go?

I fall by the integrity of what I know.

EQUINOX OF THE FLAMETHROWER

The flame's infernal cogitation,
Thinking in all directions at once,
And the thrower is a man I have come to depend on,

Pins me with heat where I stand.

I am not on fire, but I could be soon,
And what do I intend to become after I am lit?
The igniter always lingers,
And those who are scorched do not look back.

Somewhere on earth a candle mellows a face with light
As a man loves a woman,
And all the great heat in the world is aligned.

Perhaps only my hair catches
Fire, an anthem around the rest of me,
And the thrower is not responsible
For the choices I've made
To burn.

EARLY THIS MORNING

Early this morning as I walked down my street,
a sparrow flew so near, she grazed the side of my cheek
with her wing, as though I'd been singled out for a blessing.
I could approach this event any number of ways:
I could decide this was not happenstance,
but an extreme example of unmitigated trust,
the kind of faith that's almost indecent,
paralyzing in its honesty.
But I am wary of any creature
who would sacrifice so much for so little.
I could convince myself the incident
was a case of mistaken identity
wherein the bird took me to be something
I was not, a fence or a signpost perhaps,
and realizing her error,
abruptly shifted direction.
But sparrows are known for their agility,
and come rarely, if ever, so close.
I could tell myself the bird was nearly blind,
and helpless to avoid me.
But I believe she saw me
as I've never before been seen.
Perhaps she was attempting to impart a mystery
she'd kept private for too long,
to whisper to me a particular equation of leaves let go on the breeze,
a configuration only she recognizes—
how some are slower in falling,
enjoying the distance they travel to ground,
while others seem positively suicidal.
But, once again, I ascribe meaning where there was none,
and find myself faced only with the truth of what happened.
Early this morning as I walked down my street,
a sparrow flew so near, she grazed the side of my cheek
with her wing, and from this one event I understand
how easy it is to forget
to be tender.

LESSON PLAN FOR A NEW DAY

There are things the moon knows
that the sun can only imagine:
the slow, mounting gradations of light
advancing across a wet lawn in summer,
a man and woman naked at the lake's edge
alive in the warmth of each other,
believing they are hidden in darkness,
when still the moon haunts them
like a wide, translucent scarf settling over their bodies.
Were someone to ask, the sun might admit
to no more than forced brotherhood,
as the older sibling walks his sister to school
every morning, and every morning she hides,
yet he knows she is watching from under the porch,
waiting for him to turn the next corner.
I suppose were someone to press the issue
the sun might say the moon is nothing
more than a fraudulent version of itself,
an adjunct player in the cosmos,
that she answers each question with a question,
claiming nighttime is the best time for grieving.
Perhaps the moon even goes so far
as to put together a compendium
of all she has witnessed: a man murdered with a toothpick
at 2:00 A.M. on a deserted street in SoHo,
two blind people making love in a hotel room in Florence,
an owl's savage quest for food
on a midnight flight in Quebec.
Maybe she feels a primer is in order,
a lesson plan by which the sun might begin
to comprehend the distance she keeps from him,
her aloofness, always just out of reach
when the truth is: she wants him

to a point beyond which she would burn herself out
with this yearning—
when the truth is: she is less afraid to be alone
than to love him.

EPILEPSY LATE IN LIFE

Should I arrange the day around meals
Or flowers, fits,
Or talks with neighbors
I did not notice before?
Who do I credit for my gratitude?

If the moon took a name,
It would be long and difficult to pronounce.
These are the things I think about now,
By the light of what escapes me.
The constant array of hours slides the night home.

Walking through snow,
I bite my lip
To find a way
Back.

BLOOD IN THE CHOCOLATE, CHOCOLATE IN THE BLOOD

Thickness either way,
viscosity breeding itself, metallic and sweet,
sweets in dark corners of the body
where bleeding to death could be a birthday,
a personal feat, or a party
to celebrate the seasons.
Approximate the color of one, and you have the other.
Blood deepens as it ages,
and dry, the happy stain
of something sweeter.

A willingness to die is only the need for change.
Sometimes I see the sun in my dreams.
Sometimes a bank of clouds bewilder the sky,
Filled with something dark and unpronounceable—
Syrup, lead,
The moment after a person dies.

Where is the central reservoir inside the body,
The tributaries and the blood that informs them,
The silent auction which is the death of each cell?

The standards I live by are thin,
Ghosts in a room full of windows,
But someone left a truffle on one corner of the desk,
And the weight of my life is contained there.

TRANSLATION

Soon I will ask the rain where to find you,
Your quick thoughts still alive
In the seepage of an early spring.
Your birthday, and you not here to claim it.
The letters you wrote take on new prescience,
Vowels arcing high on the page
Belie an optimism you would not give up until the end.
The end—
How such small words rupture the unknown
Even as they hold it back.
Still, I am unable to translate my loss,
And the world speaks only arrival,
Running from mystery
The way water flees itself down the riverbed,
People extending themselves toward the proven, the new,
Each safe unequivocal conquest.
Time pushes its madness through every moment,
And where is the primer to unlearn this distance?

Only animals break cleanly with God.

WHITENESS

I come to you,
cold milk at the side of my mouth.
I wipe it away.
I try to forget the desire to be pure,
as you stand, tall
in a small room without a furnace,
believing only in your solitude
and the leaves
that fall in winter,
in chilly admonition of the trees.
Whiteness breaks open:
the empty bed, the sheets, fresh, folded
and calling me to them;
outside, snow like a saint's coat laid across the porch,
and my face, pale in its unknowing,
and somewhere, the white wing of a bird
maps the sky, in stillness,
in terms I have yet to translate.
The house pushes away from the frost collecting
in the rafters, the cloudy mantle of ice on the stairs,
a vacancy I will not deny.
I wipe the liquor from your lips,
brandy with a splash of milk, a ghost
in a red room.
Is it possible to recover from love
When whiteness fills the spaces between us
Allowing for nothing but itself?

ABOUT THE RIVER

I left my heart in a high place deliberately.
I wanted to see
how long I could do without it.
I wanted to see
if someone would recognize it,
and bring it back to me.
I saw where the river met the land.

I waited.

I picked up a stone and set it down
on the opposite shore
for no reason except I live
helpless in my life
and wanted much more for the stone.

I was patient.

I left my voice in a barrel,
but it rained.

I said nothing.

I left my socks so someone would worry.

I left the hat I have always worn—
I threw it into
the river and watched
it fill with water.

I saw where the river pulled away from the land.
I saw my pale skin attempt the dark,
unable to negotiate a harbor.

I left myself
as easily as a woman sets down
a thimble after sewing.
I wanted to see
how long it would take me
to realize I was missing.

I wanted to see how long
I could do without.

WOMAN WITH BREAD CRUMBS

Subversion begins with a single bird.
Anarchy when a thousand gather
To pick the ground clean,
To jar the sky open
Above the old woman's concupiscent head.

Theirs is a steady, irrefutable greed,
But in winter, the pigeons need
A saint.

She comes at five and leaves at six,
But the birds comprehend time only by the chill on the air—
How it comes
Like a man in a sinister mask;
As the sky darkens,
The mask begins to slip,
Revealing an even more hideous face.

Beneath the moon,
The ground appears featureless.
An invisible smock settles between the trees.

Things that grow remember.

Sometimes the same house revisited by lightning
Twenty years later,
Or a man with electricity in his bones
Like the tiny hiss of something alien and unforeseen,
Until one day it comes,
The rain's slow irreversible tracks nearly dissipated,
And the sky forever capable of surprise,
As the man makes his way,
Carrying a bag of nails.

If ever the truth of each human life is revealed
The way cream rises in refusal of the rest of itself,
This woman will stand on the corner,
The crumbs going soft in her hand,
And for a moment she is set apart from the world
And does not think of us,
Not even once.

AND THE PAPER, AND THE PEN

"There's no poetry between us," said the paper to the pen,
but the pen, river-bound, unquenchable, held fast above it,
and the paper found its voice in empty space,
and the pen worked harder than before, stuck in fierce circles,
spilling color on the dead air,
to touch down,
and the paper slept in its white river,
and the pen began to lose parts of itself,
darkening needles, slivers of ink
piled up along the shores
of the paper,
and the paper never moved,
each corner pointed at a distant sun,
and the pen had let so much go between itself and the paper
which did not receive it,
that nothing could be sucked back in,
and the paper needed it that way,
and the pen dried in silence,
and the paper never learned the word for itself.

INSCRIPTIONS IN A DARK ROOM

Write something here where
I will never see it,
on the underbelly of a tree frog,
a private missive in the toe of a sock,
your language balled up, sequestered
from the hand that wrote it:
I want you, but I will not allow myself
to move.
Proposing marriage into the neck of a bottle,
the condensation will make known you care.
Traces of you everywhere, but not:
a pressureless handshake,
an eyelash on the breeze.
I run my hands over your shirts,
hoping the threads will unravel,
to spell clearly your intentions,
the fabric so close to your heart.
Love letters in invisible ink.
Hate mail that just falls away.
Should I leave a stack of paper by your door,
or a small bag filled with air?

MISTAKES

Stakes. In the ground.
Not a well. Not a fence.
Each vertical lie rising up to the clouds.
Outside my window in the freezing rain
And the sun that returns
Like a hand on my back.
Stakes.
Nothing to build a house with,
Or keep the dogs in.
Driven long through the mud,
And the hammer laid here on my desk.
Stakes. No family dinner.
No meat on the plate.
Some people see them,
Straight against the arc of the sky,
But what will they do?
They respond to fury,
A hard downward swing,
The need to keep going despite
The hole,
The fractured asylum of the ground.
Don't ask how the world breaks up underneath.
Stakes. Lean and unfinished.
Sometimes stakes are not enough,
And I miss how hard I worked
To line them up.
I miss the point,
The essential vanquished moment.
I miss what I killed,
The delirium of not knowing
How far and long I have tried,
And the stakes, backlit in twilight,
Dark bones against the sky.

MY FATHER'S PEN

Never sought anguish in the ink.
Never noticed the gold was so weary.

Ideas broke from my fingers,
And I put them away.
Questions faltered at the nib.

Never thought to pick it up.
Never held it diagonally across my palm,
Or offered it to someone
To take down an address,
Or the name of a prospective lover.

I taught myself to live without it,
Burned all the papers in my house,
The pen's slender torso pulsing for years in the dark of the desk,
Evacuated of its ink.

Never held the inscription up to the light:
"1966," one year before I was born.
He was young once,
The fate of his life held back,
Acrimony, still the dream of his future.

ARTISTIC CHILDREN BREATHE DIFFERENTLY

Jenny draws giraffes with her tongue as she sleeps,
And Alan memorized all the necessary parts
To build a rocket.
Some children inspire flowers with their eyes,
And as the spit balls land in their hair,
They know what must be done.

Parents listen to their breathing with stethoscopic greed.
Send them away!
Sentence them to part-time work at the slaughter house,
Every day like grafting a hammer to the back of the skull.

How will the children outlive their fear?
With a pencil.
With paint cracking behind their voices,
They articulate cities in the emptiness of something common,
Poised to hold our human grief.

But can they extract gratitude from a lemon?
Perhaps,
Though they've stored too much loss already,
And can go no further.

Listen to the children breathe,
Trying to save themselves in their sleep.

Send them pansies, violets, wisteria vines—
All the self-slaughtered children—
Send them your sleeves
For apple-sized tears to soak into—
Send them pieces of history to learn from,
One slice of the tempest,
A bruise on the thigh of the boy-king
For luck.

AGAINST PARENTING

Fathers are the Gods of false light,
Givers of empty barrels, scratched insignia—
The cufflinks just fall to the floor.

A mother might only be worth a sack of rice.
Autumn accumulates behind her eyes,
And the faces of her children cannot replace
The footlights she thought would find her.

Children have no choice but to steal the future
And dismember the past; they arrive
With blockbuster need,
And no one can help them—not the pool man
Scraping muck from the grate;
Not the skater sluicing the ice like raw meat;
Not the poet whose obligation it is to die
For everyone all the time.

The child knows no obligation but to grow,
To outwit the envy of his parents,
To piece the puzzle back into itself
Toward a bright, singular image of self preservation,
Stoic and wise as a tree.

I WOULD LIKE TO MARRY YOU, BUT I WON'T

The cliff is steep and outrageous,
and I'm wearing the same shoes I've always worn.
I think right now marrying you would be a mistake,
though perhaps it will always be so
like a table missing a castor.
Still, we sit here, albeit at this odd angle,
your coffee cup dangerously nearing the edge,
my toast, one quick lunge from the spaniel's mouth.
I would like to marry you, but a worm lives
behind your eyes, and behind mine too,
a terror from another time, a fugitive nightmare
that has finally settled.
I would like to marry, but the world is smaller than it appears,
and I might tempt you into deeper seclusion,
the sand gather at your feet
as though to prevent your departure,
and you might say I am responsible,
that our marrying was a means by which you lost yourself,
the fragile stem of your life growing now into shadow.
I would like to marry,
not because I sympathize with the moon,
how she lives with so much wisdom
though no one reaches her, and no one tries,
but because I may never again see myself
so clearly in another person, my desire,
everything that falls from me
measured in your voice and in your eyes.
I would like to marry another man
so I might divorce him, swiftly, without regrets,
knowing you are out there still,
standing by a lake,
or arranging your hair with a slender comb,

and I would come to you then
as to a darkening sky, haunted,
alive with the surreptitious movements of the owl.

QUEEN ANNE CHERRIES

Tiny, crimson buttocks—
I leave one on your pillow,
hoping to inspire you to love.
What if my life was founded on a cherry?
What if my parents met in the grocery store,
my father picking through the cherry bin,
my mother, one aisle over, laughing at the private joke
she tells herself when she feels low.
She has a sudden craving for cherries,
and making her way to the produce section, sees my father,
who steps aside to let her at them.
The problem is he prefers Bing Cherries,
and she Queen Anne.
Still, the simple fact they like cherries at all
seems enough to carry them through.
Shiny, blood-soaked—
I place one in my mouth,
hoping to inspire you to kiss me
deeply enough to retrieve it.
What if I owe my life to a cherry?
What if my parents agreed for one night only
to put aside their bias', indulging the other's appetite,
and this is how I was created?
Burnished, slightly demented—
I swallow the stone,
hoping to inspire you to do the same.
What if I am nothing more than the product of a momentary craving?
What if my parents were meat-eaters all this time
and never let on?

POTS

The measure of love is always faith:
That day, standing by the rosebush,
I saw a sparrow fall out of the sky,
And I opened my hand.
And now pots,
Two of them, and a skillet
For braising meat,
And the sixty eyes of the colander,
And this spoon's long neck bowing
In and out of steaming water.

He gave them to me.

I find my face in the curvature of steel
As I wash it, and I try
To impart a blessing,
To understand finally
That when a man gives pots
In place of words,
He is saying the future found him,
And in that
Lies hope.

APPLES IN MY HEART

I may never find love
Apples bump together bruising
To rot
People smell what I try
Not to show
I would bake a pie but

Macintosh rolling along
Pippins in the aorta
Delicious breaking up in the blood

A man tried to kiss me but
The sweetness was a stench
Friends say I speak lush lugubrious nonsense
Sugar to the head
My toes break off in crystals

Did this happen early or late
Mid-range or far away
Alone in the hemorrhaging crowd
Or at the center of a party

Some roll north to my brain
A few south to the toes
I can't think
I can't walk

Apples on the table in a basket

You probably think that I am lying

WONDERFUL

Wonder has vacated the rest of itself,
leaving a fullness behind.
The last three letters blunder by beheaded,
and *wonder* cut down at the waist.
But I've called a meeting,
slung a thin, transparent thread
to bring the two together.

How wonderful.

Wonder knows something's gone missing,
scours the streets in silence, unable to pronounce
the true weight of itself.
How will things ever be solid again?

I am full of *wonder* at the sight of me
in the window, alone, preposterous,
trying in the late hour to unhook my blood,
from the people I betrayed,
and it's so
pure
this attempt to be honest.

Without *wonderful*, how will the world go on?
And the man I've stung over and over,
like a bison, bloated and felled on the open plain,
just lies there.

ONLY THE RUPTURED EYE SEES WHAT MUST BE DONE

A tree grew in my path,
so I took out an axe
to cut it down,
feeling its green turn to brown even as I stood there.

I've had my ocular crisis,
And now it's no longer the colors I blame,
But the shapes of men's faces,
The distance between the ears,
Or the mouth, two pieces of the same canyon.
Foreheads rise towards a premonition,
But the eyes remain focused
On a fleeting particle of light.

The sun is not a monument to God
Or the lucid eye of the lion thrown into the sky,
And when it turns dark,
The absence of light is nothing but the wish to be seen.

Watching as police probe the night for the bodies of children
In the black waters of the suburbs,
The eye has its needle already inside it.

JUST MAYBE

Maybe the world is afraid of grief.
Don't get me wrong—I don't say this to be funny
since I am not a person who takes myself that seriously,
who preaches to even the tiniest ant in the field
purposefully carrying its mountain of bread on its back
as though that one crumb could determine
the fate of the world,
but then again, maybe it can—
maybe the intricacies of desire,
the shadows that creep up in the wake of my trying,
my half-hearted attempts to ascribe some meaning
to a peach, a petunia,
the velocity of the blood
with its causeways and sudden crushing depths,
or the secret, intensely private life of the onion—
maybe grief is the best place to begin to describe this.
I could die before I learn to speak,
and all that would remain of me, everything I valued
could be bound up and tied with a string,
and that would somehow be good enough—
perhaps not the ideal summation,
but the simplest means of sustaining my faith
in what I believed might be possible.
Perhaps grief is the recollection
not of what went missing, but of everything
in its rightful place.
I once saw a man pass me on the street.
In the middle of the sidewalk was a snail
crossing with the kind of heartbreaking deliberation
found only in nature.
I was careful to step over it
while the man who passed me turned around,
walked back and crushed the snail with the heel of his shoe.

Never have I witnessed such staggering efficiency,
as though nothing else mattered
but to rid the world of something more devoted than himself.
Perhaps that man was afraid of his grief,
and in that instant he perceived the snail
to be the slow-moving vessel of his own self-loathing.
Somehow everything he could not name within himself
was inching its way across his path,
and he was helpless to prevent its finding him.

THE NEED FOR EVERYTHING

I've always been wary of endings—
my mother's sweeping gesture, her hand
decapitating the air to drive home a point.
I've always been afraid of my craving for beauty,
to make clear what I see, if only to myself,
which would be safe
since no one would have to know
I noticed the curve of the whippet's back
like a scythe as he lowered his head to drink,
or the way my father sits, childlike,
fingers interlaced across his lap.
The expression on his face betrays understanding.
I have always made an effort
never to wear blue in the company of the desperately sad.
Still, sometimes I find myself standing in an indigo sweater,
looking into a window—suddenly stunned my own reflection,
and by the time I finally catch myself,
I am weeping.
I am thankful for the unexpected:
the confiscated beauty of a butterfly,
pinned and transfixed under glass.
Day after day the need for everything fills me.
I will send fifty cents to help save the whales.

CHOPPING WALNUTS

This is the way I say goodbye,
Pulling them like wooden moths from the bag,
Laying each one on the table, to chop,
Until the soft pulpy mountain is made.
My mother asks me to do this for her,
And it seems so unimportant,
The smallness of the gesture falling so short of love,
But maybe love is only the respect we have for each other
And the things we need done at the end.
I fold the towels, lifting them to their proper shelf.
I move through the house as though I were part of a painting
Of a house on a hill in a town
No one remembers.
The curtains shift frame by frame, in increments,
And I walk to the door without ever moving.
Death is not a huge, strapping moment,
But the slow unwinding of a scarf
My mother wore in spring,
And will not come back to.

WORDS BEFORE LEAVING

You said the world lumbers,
turning like a fat, ugly wheel,
and no one cares, you said,
that someone's childhood
was starving
well into her thirty-fifth year, you said,
there was too much to do
in this slowness keeping up with itself,
and then you said a bird dies
and people step over it,
and another thing orphaned
and another and another, you said
the nations don't care
who is ugly, how each person fights
against his own fate,
and in winter, the air
rips its cold polemic through the trees,
you said I should take better care
of the things I can count on,
and the stranger who stops to tie his shoelace
in the middle of the street
and does not see what is coming
is still a stranger,
and water rises
and people don't care
to close the space
between themselves and each other,
and you said all this
as I was leaving.

THE TRUE MEANING OF YES

The restraints have been lifted,
Yes, an allocation, liquefied,
Let loose into the world to spread
Its equanimity into holes, thimbles
Where brackish water collects,
And small birds wait their turn to drink,
Beyond the insufferable weight of doors
And the rooms they defend
To unfold finally like a bridge.

Yes is the breath of animals
Where the inadmissible gives no verdict in the voice,
And the moose only bellows
For her body to be sated.

Write the word on your palm
And it will influence the way you greet a stranger.
Bell's toll their *yes'* every hour,
And no is only the absence of sound.

Yes waits buried in the mouth's constant dark,
Awaiting excavation.
Say it.
Give the word as a gift,
As though pronouncement would grant it a body,
To graze your cheek with the back of a hand
Or summon you closer.

www.ingramcontent.com/pod-product-compliance
Lightning Source LLC
Chambersburg PA
CBHW022346040426
42449CB00006B/737